Walruses

Victoria Blakemore

Copyright info/picture credits

Cover, Amelie Koch/Shutterstock; Page 3, Incredible Arctic/AdpbeStock; Page 5, Vladimir Melnik/AdobeStock; Page 7, Amelie Koch/Shutterstock; Page 9, Victoria Lipov/AdobeStock; Pages 10-11, Patrick Poendl/AdobeStock; Page 13, stockphoto mania/AdobeStock; Page 15, misterfarmer/Pixabay; Page 17, amheruko/AdobeStock; Page 19, stockphoto mania/AdobeStock; Page 21, roman_kharlamov/AdobeStock; Page 23; Hal Brindley/AdobeStock; Page 25, Vladimir Melnik/AdobeStock; Page 27, PIXATERRA/AdobeStock; Page 29, outdoorsman/AdobeStock; Page 31, bambur/AdobeStock; Page 33, MAK/AdobeStock

Table of Contents

What Are Walruses?

Walruses are a special kind of mammal known as a **pinniped**. They have flippers instead of feet.

There are two kinds of walruses: the Pacific walrus and the Atlantic walrus. They are named for the ocean they are found in.

Walruses are large and usually brown in color.

Size

Walruses can grow to be about twelve feet long. Most walruses weigh between 2,000 and 3,000 pounds. Some walruses may weigh as much as 4,000 pounds.

Male walruses are usually larger than female walruses.

The Pacific walrus tends to be longer and heavier than the Atlantic walrus.

Walruses have large tusks.

Their tusks are actually large

teeth that grow much bigger

than the rest of their teeth.

They use their tusks to pull

themselves out of the water

onto the ice. Their tusks can

also be used to break

through ice.

Male walruses usually have

longer and thicker tusks than

females.

Habitat

Walruses are found along **coasts**. They prefer areas with lots of ice and water that isn't too deep. Temperatures below freezing are best for walruses.

Walruses may **migrate** as the weather gets warmer. They may go farther north as the ice melts in the south.

Range

Walruses are only found in the Arctic Circle.

They are found on the coasts of parts of Russia, Canada, Alaska, Greenland, and parts of Europe.

Diet

Walruses are **carnivores**. They

eat only meat.

Clams, snails, worms, squids,

fish, and sometimes even

seals make up the walrus

diet.

Walruses rarely chew and often swallow their food whole!

Walruses have a special way
to find food on the ocean
floor. They dive down and
blow puffs of air into the
sand.

They also use their whiskers,
to feel around for food in the
dark waters.

Walrus whiskers are very

sensitive bristles. They help

the walrus to feel prey in the

sand.

Staying Warm

Walruses have a thick layer of **blubber**, or fat, under their skin. It helps them to stay warm.

Scientists discovered that walruses can slow their hearts down. This helps them to stay warm when they are diving into icy waters.

Walruses have a layer of blubber

that can be six inches thick.

Communication

Walruses use mainly sound to communicate. They are able to make many different sounds. They can growl, grunt, bark, click, and whistle.

Male walruses have a special sound that they make under the water. It sounds like a bell.

Walruses have special air sacs in their neck. These air sacs allow them to make special sounds. They also let walruses sleep underwater!

Movement

Walruses are very slow on land. Their large size and flippers can make it hard for them to get around.

In the water, walruses are very fast swimmers. Their powerful flippers help them to glide through the water.

Walruses are great divers. They have been seen diving over 300 feet below the water's surface.

Colony Life

Walruses are very social animals, which means that they like to stay in groups.

A group of walruses is called a colony. Colonies can be made up of hundreds of walruses.

Colonies of walruses are

often seen resting together

on the ice.

Walrus Pups

Walruses have one baby, called a pup or a cub. Pups are usually gray in color. They do not have tusks when they are born.

Pups stay with their mothers until they are at least two years old.

Walrus mothers protect their

pups from **predators** like polar

bears and orcas.

Life Span

In the wild, walruses have been known to live up to forty years. Once they are fully grown, they are safe from most predators.

Walrus pups are sometimes hunted by polar bears and orcas.

Male walruses are sometimes

hurt in fights with other walruses.

Population

There are believed to be about 250,000 walruses in the wild. Walruses were close to becoming **extinct** in the 1930's.

Laws were passed in many countries to stop people from hunting walruses.

Walruses have been hunted by humans for their meat, skin, and tusks.

Helping Walruses

Walrus populations have grown in recent years. People want to make sure that walruses are not in danger of extinction again.

Researchers are studying walrus populations. They want to have an **accurate** count of how many are in the wild.

Temperatures in the Arctic have been getting warmer. This is causing ice to melt, which is not good for walruses.

There are groups that are trying to help walruses. They want to try to stop the change in temperature so that walrus habitats are not destroyed.

Glossary

Accurate: correct, free of mistakes

Blubber: fat that keeps animals warm

Carnivore: an animal that eats meat

Coast: where the land meets the ocean

Extinct: when there are no more

of an animal left

Migrate: to travel from one

place to another

Pinniped: a mammal that has

flippers instead of feet

Predator: an animal that hunts

other animals for food

About the Author

Victoria Blakemore is a first grade

teacher in Southwest Florida with a

passion for reading.

You can visit her at

www.elementaryexplorers.com

Also in This Series

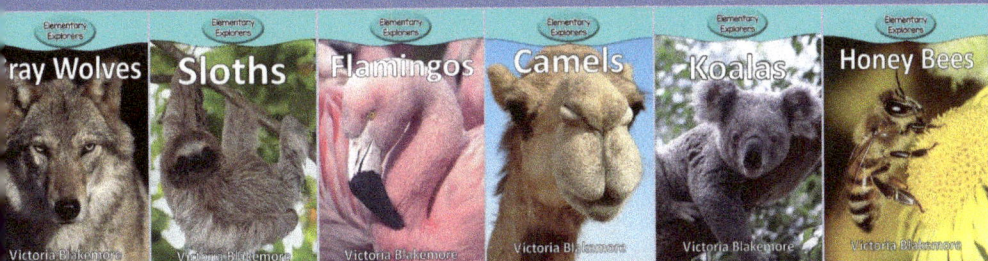

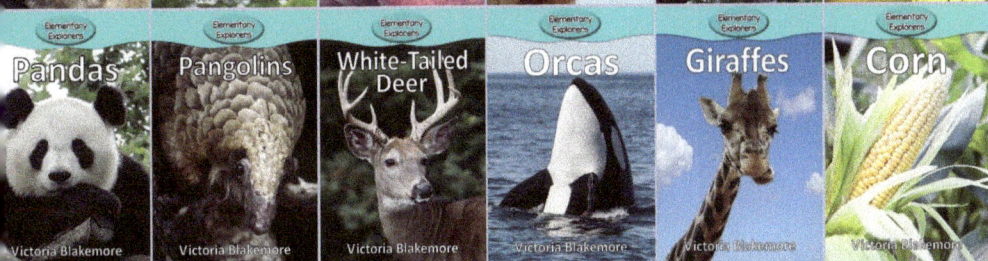

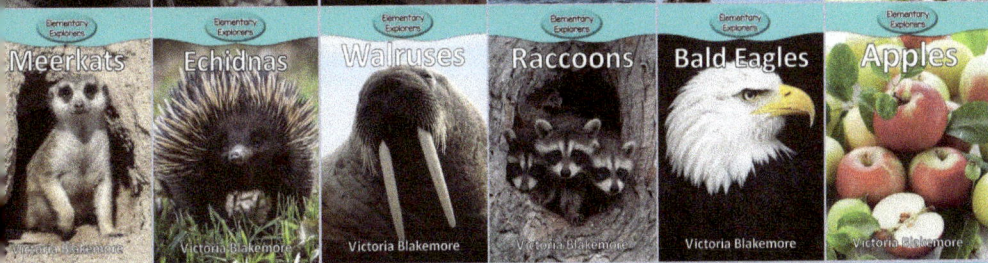

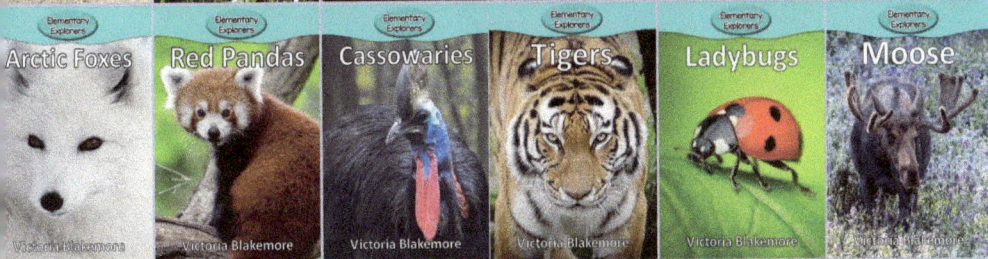

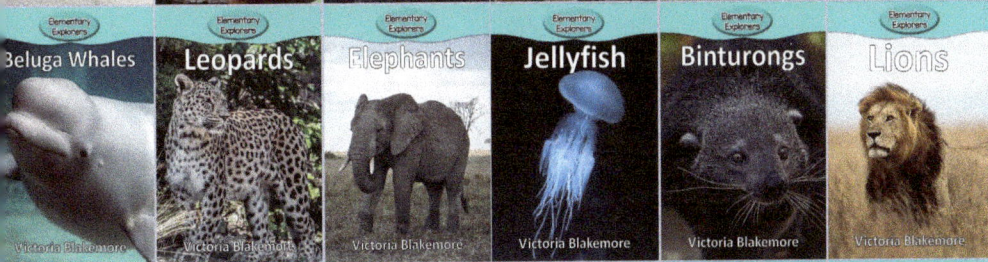

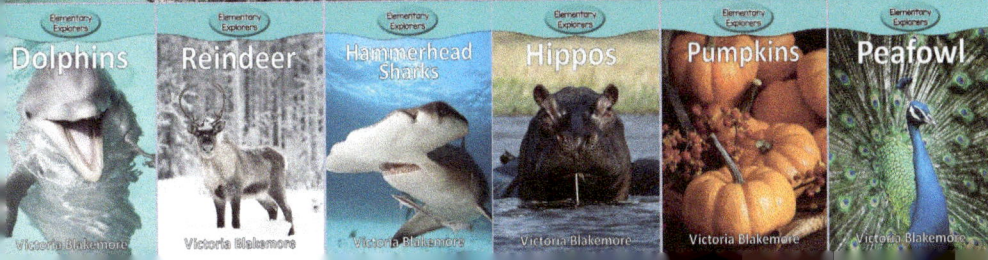

Gray Wolves · Sloths · Flamingos · Camels · Koalas · Honey Bees

Pandas · Pangolins · White-Tailed Deer · Orcas · Giraffes · Corn

Meerkats · Echidnas · Walruses · Raccoons · Bald Eagles · Apples

Arctic Foxes · Red Pandas · Cassowaries · Tigers · Ladybugs · Moose

Beluga Whales · Leopards · Elephants · Jellyfish · Binturongs · Lions

Dolphins · Reindeer · Hammerhead Sharks · Hippos · Pumpkins · Peafowl

Victoria Blakemore

Also in This Series

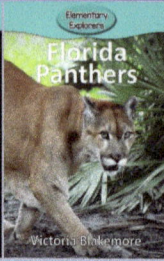

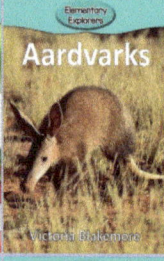

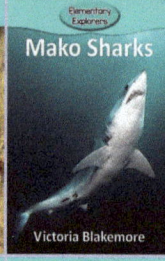

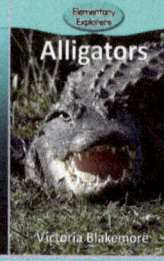

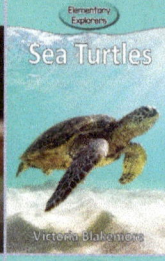

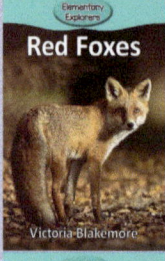

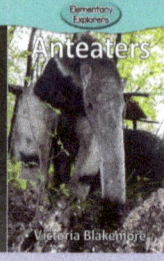

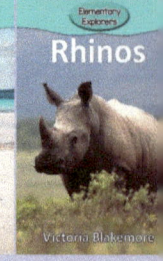

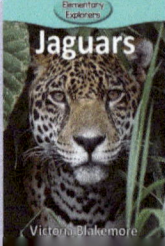

Elementary Explorers
Chameleons
Victoria Blakemore

Elementary Explorers
Florida Panthers
Victoria Blakemore

Elementary Explorers
Aye-Ayes
Victoria Blakemore

Elementary Explorers
Black Bears
Victoria Blakemore

Elementary Explorers
Cheetahs
Victoria Blakemore

Elementary Explorers
Manatees
Victoria Blakemore

Elementary Explorers
Gingerbread
Victoria Blakemore

Elementary Explorers
Polar Bears
Victoria Blakemore

Elementary Explorers
Hot Chocolate
Victoria Blakemore

Elementary Explorers
Orangutans
Victoria Blakemore

Elementary Explorers
Coyotes
Victoria Blakemore

Elementary Explorers
Marshmallow
Victoria Blakemore

Elementary Explorers
Strawberries
Victoria Blakemore

Elementary Explorers
Aardvarks
Victoria Blakemore

Elementary Explorers
Mako Sharks
Victoria Blakemore

Elementary Explorers
Alligators
Victoria Blakemore

Elementary Explorers
Frogs
Victoria Blakemore

Elementary Explorers
Hedgehogs
Victoria Blakemore

Elementary Explorers
Brown Bears
Victoria Blakemore

Elementary Explorers
Bongos
Victoria Blakemore

Elementary Explorers
Sea Turtles
Victoria Blakemore

Elementary Explorers
Quokkas
Victoria Blakemore

Elementary Explorers
Muskrats
Victoria Blakemore

Elementary Explorers
Zebras
Victoria Blakemore

Elementary Explorers
Red Foxes
Victoria Blakemore

Elementary Explorers
Ring-Tailed Lemurs
Victoria Blakemore

Elementary Explorers
Platypuses
Victoria Blakemore

Elementary Explorers
Anteaters
Victoria Blakemore

Elementary Explorers
Kangaroos
Victoria Blakemore

Elementary Explorers
Rhinos
Victoria Blakemore

Elementary Explorers
Jaguars
Victoria Blakemore

Elementary Explorers
Wombats
Victoria Blakemore